Sunflower Love

– Dezz

Wider Perspectives Publishing
ISBN: 978-1-952773-15-0

Acknowledgment

If a sunflower can not find the sun,
it gravitates towards another sunflower
Not all sunflowers are yellow
The yellow ones are just well known
When my head was low, cuz I'm a shade of purple
You reminded me that I am still a sunflower
That I still hold connection to Apollo
That I am full of seeds that need planting
When I lost my sun
You gave me someone to reach for
Something to hold on to
When I found my sun again
You were still there supporting
Just wanting to see how tall I'd grow to be
And that means nothing short of the world to me

Contents

To Bask in The Sun

I've Loved You Before

You're so familiar
Like home.
Not the one I came from
The one I intend to build

When our lips first kissed
They didn't say "nice to meet you"
They said "Nice to see you again"
Said "Took you long enough, where have you been?"
Said "You came back to me"
Said "I missed you"

They laughed at the ones we have kissed before
Cause our lips always knew
I've loved you before
I mean I just had to

Forever

I don't think I'm built for forever
Forever scares me
I can plan for forever
Life can have other plans

I don't Know how to handle forever
It makes me anxious
Self sabotage
From fear this is just a mirage

I can't give you forever
But if you can spare 5 minutes
I can give you that

I can give you the next 5 minutes of my life
We can just look into each other's eyes
Or at the night sky
You can tell me about your family
Your hopes and dreams
Everything...you can fit in 5 minutes

Forever might scare you too.
All I ask is the next five minutes
If we lose track of time
If it begins to fly
We'll stop it
Ask for the next five minute
The next five minutes till sunset
Sunrise
The next 5 minutes for the rest of our lives

I don't think I'm built for forever
But I will give you all the next 5 minutes I have to offer

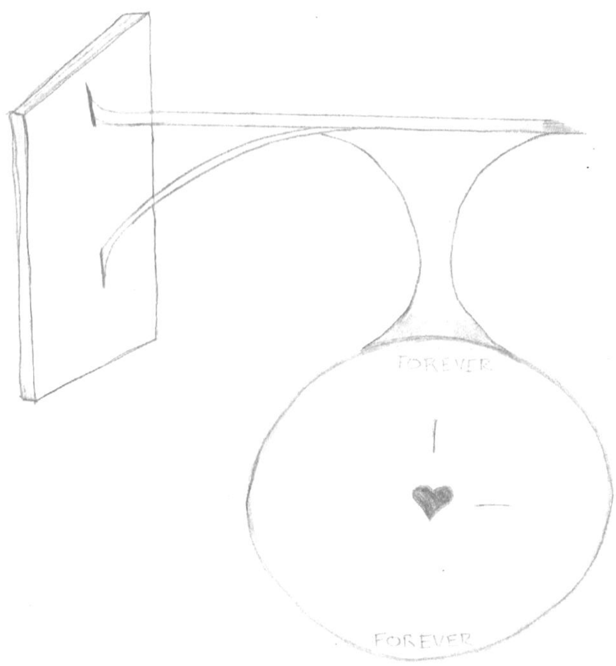

Foolish

You make for bad poetry

Once you decided to replace my lonely with happy
You came to the conclusion that it's alright, by "it" I
mean the way you look at me
I do believe you like to see me melting

You stole it, my heart
You took it without permission
This is not a play I got no intermission
Where I could gather my thoughts, sort through my
feelings

Feeling, what in this world is this feeling
Why did my emotions switch up so quickly
I...won't say I'm in love

What a foolish thing to say
What a foolish game to play
What a foolish person you must think I am

Why would I willingly want to give you every piece of me,
Want to tell you everything about me
The good, the bad, the ugly?

Spend my time only wanting to make sure you're happy
How foolish of me would that be?

To get attached
To have my heart ache a little bit when I'm not in your presence
I am usually smarter than this,
But you,
You make me foolish

Dezz

Home

My home smells of shea butter
Of home remedies, balanced chakras
And burning incense

Smells like rain or better yet the day after
When everything has been watered

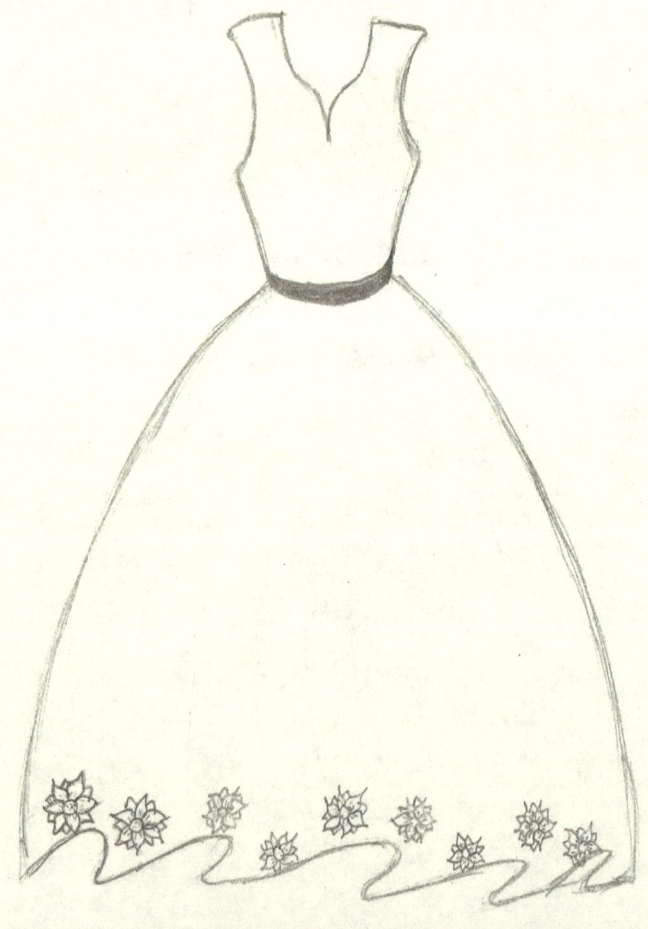

Smells like sunflowers
Smells of hard work, determination
Of progress. it's not always a lot,
But progress nonetheless

My home sounds like honey
Sounds like mountains, singing
Like windchimes on a spring day
Like laughter, the genuine kind
From your gut, no from your soul

Sounds like your heart smiling

Sometimes my home sounds like sadness
Even though there is always love in it.
Sounds like "I just need to be alone sometimes"
Like depression.....not winning
My home sounds like fighting for your happy
Not always winning, but still fighting

My home feels like, well, home
Like if freshly baked cookies could wrap themselves
around you

Feels like a weighted blanket fresh out the dryer
Like vulnerability, without the fear

Feels like growth, like a challenge
Like there's no place like home
Minus the red slippers, the murder, the me ever
Being uncertain I belong here

My home looks like big brown eyes
Full of wonder and hope for the world
Looks like subtle concentration
Looks like passion, like living your passion

My home looks like walking in your purpose
My home looks like two arms and a heartbeat

And what it tastes like.... is mine

Sunday

You remind me of that Sunday Kind of love
The Kind that Etta James said would last past
Saturday night
Sunday mornings
When my face goes from being beat to looKing beat

When my head is pounding
Yet the sound of your voice is soothing
Where we stay in bed past 11
Tryna catch the light with our fingertips
Transferring energy with a Kiss

I would never say "I get drunK on you"
That type of ecstasy only last a short amount of
time
While we

We on some forever shit
We on some Sunday morning shit
Some construction site, cuz we building shit
Some quench my thirst shit

You're Kinda like flavored water to me
I can survive without you
But you, you make life a little sweeter
I'm more excited about waking up
Knowing I get to see you

You are my Sunday afternoons
Dressed in your T-shirt
Wrapped in your arms
Breathing life into each other

Dezz's Testimony

There's something special about shea butter fingertips.
The way they feel on my skin.

They help heal the scars of the past
The ones I will never forget,
But those fingertips tell me I don't have to always remember

When I get anxious those fingertips
Hold my hand
Wrap the arms that come attached around me
Breathes with me
Sings to me

Those fingertips
They sit with me
They say "Look at me, I'm not running"
They say "You got me"
"We're growing, together"

Those fingertips remind me
Different people bring out different parts of you

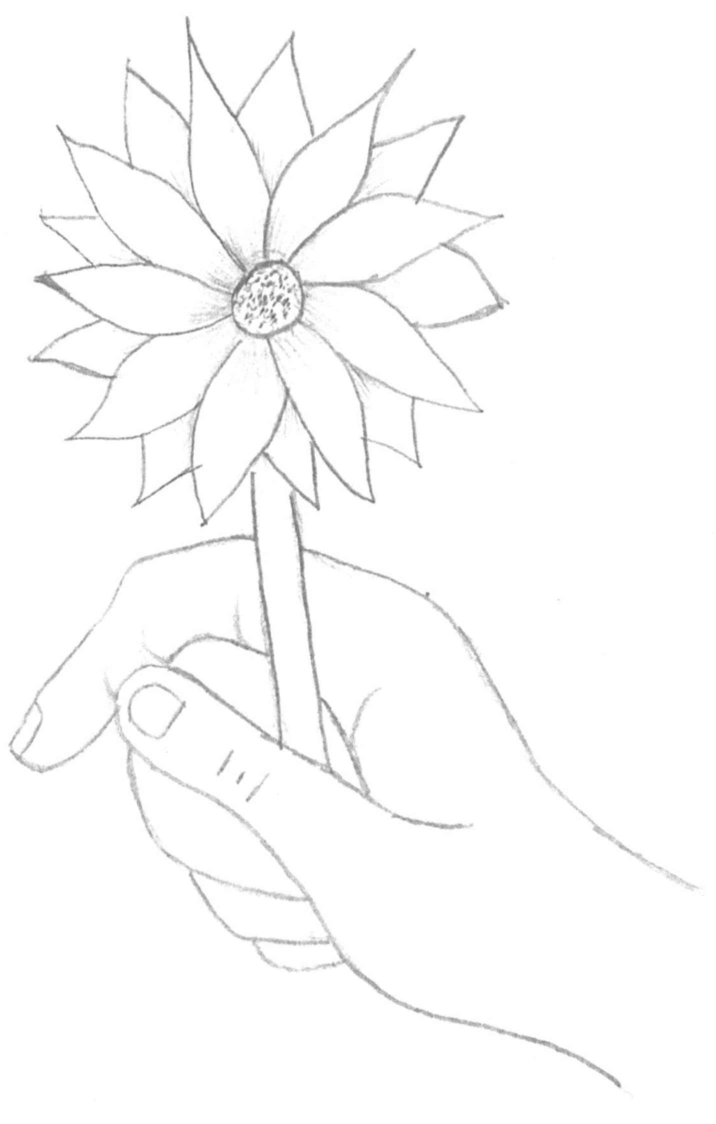

You might just be thinking, 'all of this over some fingertips...'
That's because you don't Know the heart that comes with them
The eyes
The smile
Well wishes
Cocoa butter Kisses

To Wilt

Dear God

Dear God,
I come to you with first world problems.
Considering you've done nothing about them third world problems
I doubt you'll take the time to help me,

But you see
My momma believes in you
She says if I give all things to you
You might be able to do something about it.

Question..
Adam and Eve, what happened to their relationship?

If Adam could forgive Eve
Which I'm assuming he did
Otherwise the rest of us would have never been created

Why couldn't you?
I'm assuming you didn't because my insides try to kill me monthly

Were they happy together?
Or were they simply doing their duty
Because it's your will

Speaking of your will...

What plans do you have for my broken heart?
That's a part of your will too, right?

To give me my own piece of heaven
Then snatch it away from me like it's a toy
Is that all we are to you ...toys

Dear God,

I saw your face, everytime he looked me in my eyes.
I felt your touch, every time he held my hand or hugged me.
I knew you were real, because he loved me
My God, he loved me

You might think I'm being over dramatic
But I've never felt pain like this.

I'd ask you to help me
But you're all seeing
Not only did you see it happen
You saw it coming
And still chose to do nothing

Dear God,
Are you listening?!

Dear God,
Are you listening?!

Do you even care?!

Dear God,
Dear God,
Dear God,

You said you'd never forsake me
So why does it feel like you left

When he did?

You Don't Get To....

You don't get to tell me this isn't like me
You lost all eligibility
To claim you know me
When chose to lay next to her

No, you don't get to say I'm "acting out"
I didn't throw a brick through your window
Burn all you clothes
Nor did I call your dad who told you to never disrespect a woman
Telling him that you disrespected a woman

I cut my hair because you loved it
I ripped every poem that slightly reminded me of you
Not to "act out", to become new

You don't get to tell me you miss me
Once again you're trying to feed me bullshit, I'm not hungry

You see you don't get to call me a whore
Who occupies the other half of my bed is not your concern

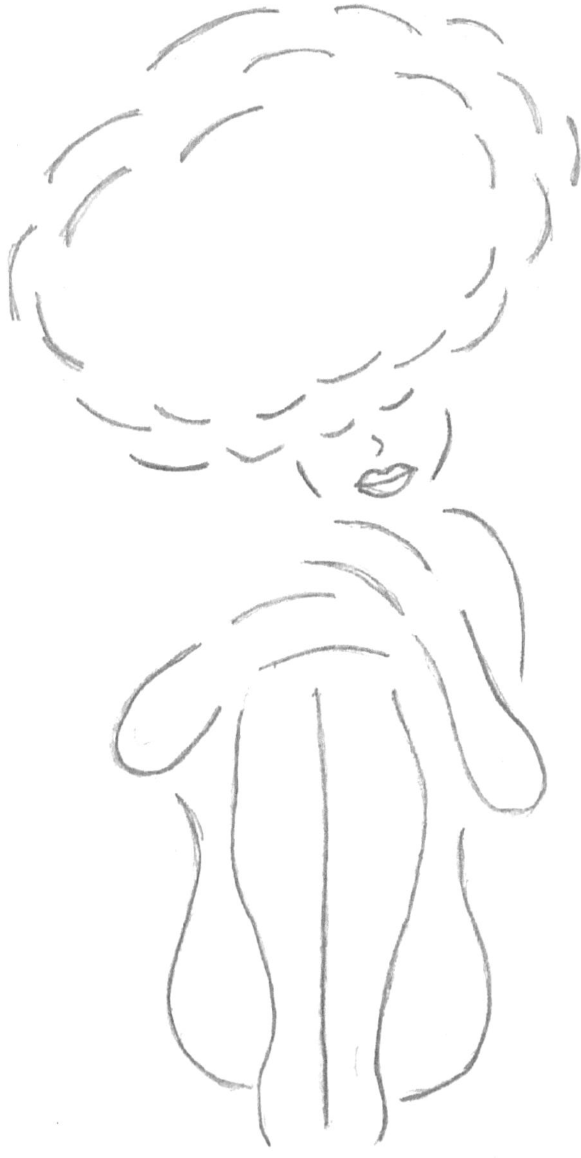

I am fixing what you broke
How I do that is up to me

If I'm the whore, you want me to be.
You made me this way
I get to be who ever it takes
To rid my memory of the time you had me waste

Good Poetry

Tell me you never want to see me again
He said "I can't"
Tell me you never want to talk to me again
He said "I can't"
Tell me that I mean nothing to you
he said "I can't"

Actions speak louder than words
So that weak ass apology you gave me
After you fucked her
Shove it up your ass
Better yet
Shove it up her vagina
Since that's where you like to put things
That are supposed to be just for me

I really wish I hated you
I would much rather hate you than admit
I gave you every piece of me
The box said fragile
You put more care into who you let cut your hair

You keep saying sorry
You're sorry does nothing for me

I wonder, If this is how Jack felt
When he realized that Rose just let him die
Instead of scooting the fuck over so he could get on the door with her

You let me drown
The water is freezing
Hey, at the end of the day
At least you make for good poetry

It's You

"It's not you, its me"

No shit Sherlock!
I have been here day in, day out giving my all to "us"
While you've been giving your all to an "us" that doesn't include me
So in reality it's not me.......it's her

You started teaching her the language that only our bodies knew
Using your fingertips to tell her curves the secrets you once told mine
And I...

Am supposed to bite my tongue so hard I form tears
In the sockets of my eyes
As you tell me some shit I already knew

You said "we've been drifting a part for a while now"
Lies!
Maybe if you weren't so busy swimming to her
You would've seen that I never moved
I stayed in the same place

I don't blame the ocean for our sinking ship
The water never would've gotten through
If you didn't, poke holes in our foundation
Inviting it

I know it's not me
I don't mean that to sound cocky
I am very aware of my flaws
I know how to apologize

The only time I lied was to cover up a surprise
The only time you lied was when it was in bed with someone else

You were gone long before you decided to leave
I completely agree
It's you, not me

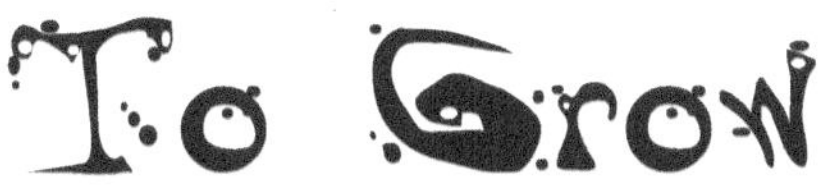
To Grow

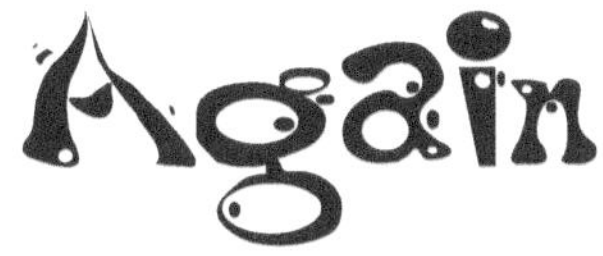
Again

Shrimp Love

Your love for me reminds me of my sister's love for shrimp
It is, after all, her favorite food

She "loves" shrimp so much
She takes it out of its natural habitat, murders it, watches as she set it's body on fire, rips it apart and devours it
Yet she....loves it

You are infatuated with the idea of love
In awe of the happily ever after tactics
That have formed in your head
Telling you, you'll find you a princess

Not every. girl is a princess
Some of us are warriors
Guardians, protectors
We don't all need saving
Or prince charming

Little boy, I am not looking for a prince to save me

I am in search of a King, because I am a queen
I wouldn't really call it searching, more like preparing
Loving every part of me
In order to make sure he does it properly

Becoming the best version of myself
When he finally comes I will be ready

I've had this epiphany
I deserve more than the love the shrimp gets
I deserve to be loved cracks included
I won't wait around for it
I'll give it to my damn self

Mistaken for Love

It was not love that hurt me
Love is not the reason it is hard for me to trust
For that was caused by betrayal

Love, has nothing to do with the tears my sheets and pillows are stained with
The ice that has formed around my heart in order to protect it
For the million and one questions I will ask
Due to the fact the I need reassurance

You see love has never hurt me
Loving the wrong person is what fucked me up

They tell you love is blind
Depending on the person it's also deaf
I had come up with my own sign language in order to defend
Your "I love you" statements

However one should not have to defend their love
For defense should already be present
In your eyes, your touch, your actions
Your actions
Actions!

Love has never hurt me
It was letting myself be deceived, by myself that
fucked me up
Lying to myself to make things "OK"
Saying things like "This is just a phase"

Love has never hurt me
It was falling with no one to catch me that fucked
me up

It was putting the task of my happiness on someone
else that fucked me up
The thing that comes after love
When love dies
Or when the love was lies
There is nothing wrong with love
It's a beautiful thing
It's all the things mistaken for love, that fucks us
up.

Dime

If I had a dime
For every time someone has fucked me over
I'd be rich

If I had a dime
For every time I tried to see the good in somebody
Who didn't deserve that from me
I swear I'd be out of debt

But I'm not
Cuz I don't
All I have is the poem created from broken pieces of
a wounded heart

You've mistreated me
Taken me for granted
Time and time again

Honestly, if I had a boat and you were drowning...

I'd save you
With no hesitation
No recognition needed

I refuse to let anyone taint my spirit
everybody needs somebody

We don't all deserve somebody
That has never stopped us from needing them

While ones energy needs to be protected
If it the right Kind, it can be infectious
So if I had a boat and you were drowning...
I'd save you

I was taught to leave things better than I find them
Once I leave you

I'll hope
That after me
You're heart will be softer
You'll be Kinder
More open to trying new things

I hope I made my presence evident
Leaving some Kind of evidence

When you remember me
Remember I only ever wanted the best for you
But, I want the best for me too

S.O.G.V.

The story of the grape vine
Says something about you wanting to buy me all the cheddar cheese biscuits I can eat.

Tells of the seed you planted
That sprouted and made its way to me

Speaks on how I was stuck in my cycles
Until you took aim, like a sharpshooter
And snapped me out of it
It's like I was in a deep sleep
The only thing I heard was you saying
"You gotta wake up"

It reads that now I'm in a new cycle
A cycle of healing
But I can't help but wonder
If this garden of mine will ever grow
I get this half empty feeling when it comes to the unknown
You see, tomorrow ain't promised and today is kinda a mess

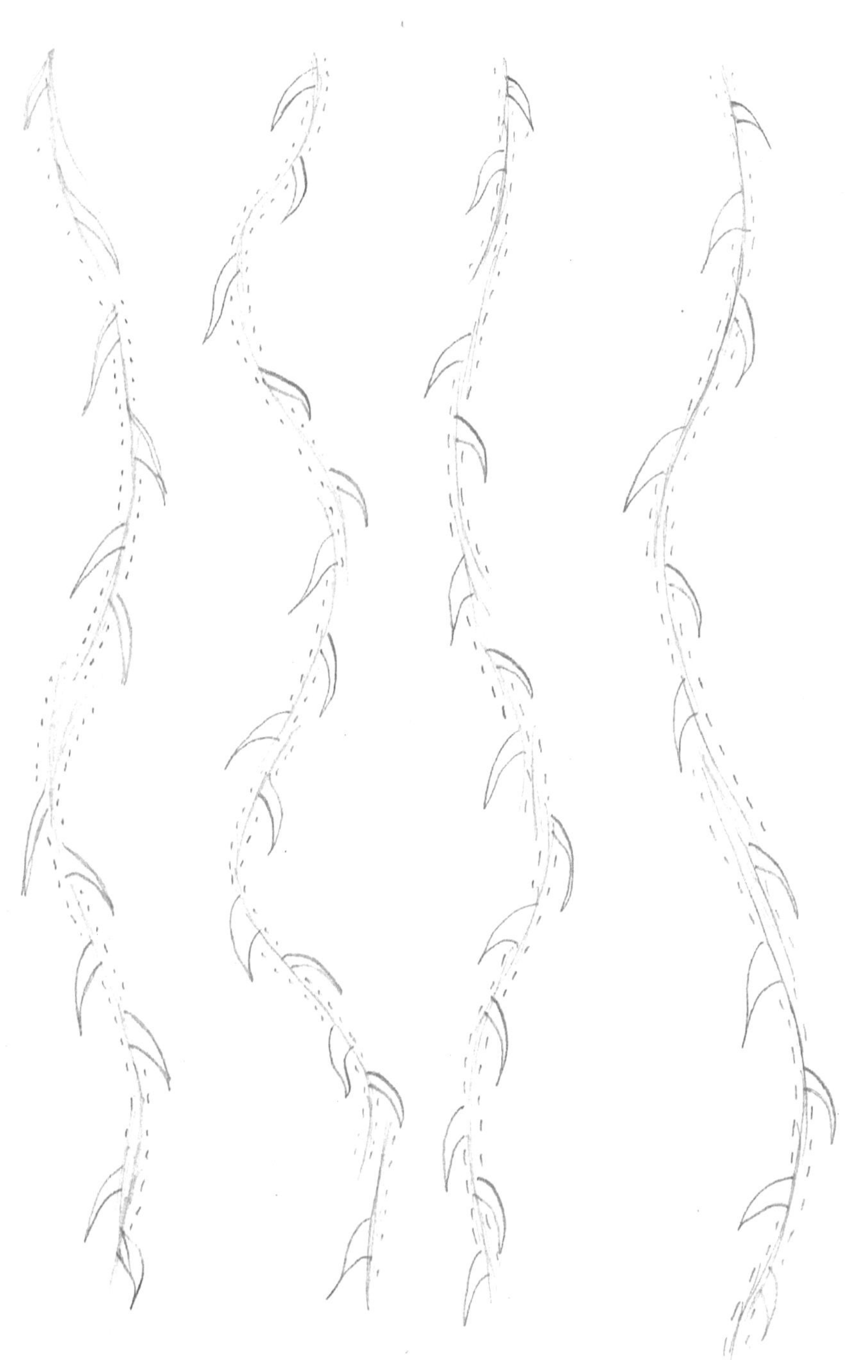

The story of the grape vine
Mentions third eye Kisses
How when they come from you
I get a different Kind of vision
Like I'm something of a profit
Takes me out of the self doubt
I was waist deep in

I'm leaning fully into my demi-god potential
Tired of being treated like some Kind of animal
Tapping into every power that be... in me

The story of the grape vine will tell of your strength
It will say how you have inspired and continue to
inspire people
It will sing Testimony
It will preach peace

And I....I will listen woefully
Just happy that I'm here to see it all happen
Cuz man, it's gonna be quite the story

My Pen

(NorfolK)

My pen is NorfolK
My pen is park place
Is the venue on 35th st, watergate cuisine, TWP, cipher Tuesday's

My pen is pancaKes by Sarah
Watching bad movies with Jorge
SmacK talKing by Bridges
Outside conversations with Issa

My pen is full of "I Know you" "I'm proud of you" "dats my baby"

My pen is also full of "Slam Richmond donated a special place and we call it...the fucK out side, that way... with yo rude ass"

My pen is me reciting a poem and crying
God Child sayin' he got me
People telling me they got me and for the first time in a long time me believing it

My pen is asking Shanna where she got her outfits
Knowing that she's prays for me

My pen is life advice and warm hugs from Momma D
Is car Karaoke with my babies
Blasting Marv. P
Is teaching, learning, and listening

My pen is memes from Q5....daily

My pen is loving and being loved
And sharing that Testimony

My pen is Andre
Is heartbreak
Is still love
Is still support
Is still your biggest fan

My pen is D, e, double Z
Cuz I'm a little extra, or so I've been told

My pen is Norfolk
And when someone says "well you're not from Norfolk"
I respond, "but my pen sure as hell is"

colophon

Brought to you by Wider Perspectives Publishing, care of James Wilson, with the mission of advancing the poetry and creative community of Hampton Roads, Virginia.

See our production of works from ...

Edith Blake
Terra Leigh
Ray Simmons
Samantha Borders-Shoemaker
Taz Waysweete'
Bobby K. (The Poor Man's Poet)
J. Scott Wilson (TEECH!)
Charles Wilson
Gloria Darlene Mann
Neil Spirtas
Jorge Mendez & JT Williams
Sarah Eileen Williams
Stephanie Diana (Noftz)
the Hampton Roads Artistic Collective
Jason Brown (Drk Mtr)
Martina Champion
Tony Broadway
Ken Sutton
Crickyt J. Expression
Lisa M. Kendrick
Cassandra IsFree
Nich (Nicholis Williams)
Samantha Geovjian Clarke
Natalie Morison-Uzzle
Gus Woodward II
Shanya (Lady S)

... and others to come soon.

We promote and support the artists of the 757

from the seats, from the stands,
from the snapping fingers and
clapping hands
from the pages, and the stages
and now we pass them forth
to the ages

Check for the above artists on FaceBook, the Virginia Poetry Online channel on YouTube, and other social media.

Hampton Roads Artistic Collective is the non-profit extension of WPP and strives to simultaneously support worthy causes in Hampton Roads and the creative artists.

www.ingramcontent.com/pod-product-compliance
Lightning Source LLC
LaVergne TN
LVHW051021080826
845145LV00009B/2737

* 9 7 8 1 9 5 2 7 7 3 1 5 0 *